To

From

Before he is born
he is an astonishment,
a nervous speculation.
He is born –
and he is an amazement,
a perfection.

He opens his eyes,
looks at you and you know
he is already his own person –
and a small shiver of wonder
runs through you.

Babies and parents
teach one another
how to love.

Babies are delighted
that you're delighted.
And you're delighted that they are.
Which is one of the most
satisfactory states
known to humankind.

The day you

become a parent...

You grow suddenly in strength
and dignity.
In love. In tenderness.
The newborn child so small,
is safe in your arms

You are so very small,
so wonderfully made.
You will grow into the world and learn
and change
– but I will always recognize the child
whose hands I hold
today.
And love the person that you are
and will become.

Time

for a cuddle

Time for a song.
Time for a talk.
Three o'clock in the morning?
What's time to friends?

Babies master the art o

ooking cute very early on.

One looks at a sleeping baby – and forgives it everything.

Watching him grow

A baby son is a mystery.
His parents watch him grow with pride,
with puzzlement and with delight.
Go on astonishing us!
We wish you courage
and hope and curiosity. And love.

It's been an awful day.
Rain. Bills. Flu.
But the baby smiles
– and it's all forgotten.

We've waited for him so long
and now he's here.
More beautiful than we ever dreamed.
More wonderful. More precious.

He's yours

This little child is brand new –
to the family, to the world,
to the universe.
Nothing quite like him has ever
existed before.
He is a new beginning –
An astonishment.
And he is yours.

A gift beyond price.

To find yourself
accepted by a baby, and see him
smile at you –
is a gift beyond price.

Through a child's eyes
we rediscover the world's loveliness
and mystery.

Whilst so small and helpless
this child needs every ounce
of your care and protection.
Later on he will need your guidance
and advice.
And one day, before you are ready,
he will need you to let go.
But needing your love?
That will be for always.

The steel-strong, web-fine links
that bind sons
to those who love them
and whom they love in turn,
cannot be broken.

To the end